I Love You More

A collection of Memories

Kat Wren

BookLeaf Publishing

India | USA | UK

Dedication

To my grandmother,
Her love will live on with us.

Preface

"I Love You More" was the last thing my grandmother said to me. This phrase was a bit of a competition between us, our thing that we did. The goal was always simple: to be the first to say it when we saw each other, and sometimes, we got very creative through Christmas gifts or TV shows. Other times it would be one of us screaming it louder than the other. Either way, it would always bring a smile to our faces and sometimes laughs or groans of frustration at losing. But like all good things, it came to an end a week before we lost her. I was saying goodbye because I had to head home for work but planned to be back down the following weekend to see her. The look in her eyes as she said smiled softly and won one last time will forever be ingrained into my memory. So, since I didn't get to say it back, I hope this can be a reply of some kind.

Acknowledgements

Thank you to my family and friends who have always supported me. And a special thank you to my grandmother for always being there and treating me like one of her own.

Living Nightmare

A tight knot forms with my every breath as I remember that night. The house was quiet...it was odd...it's never quiet. But the soft beat from my headphones kept me from any overwhelming thoughts as we wait...unknowingly waiting...yet knowing it wasn't a good day...not for her...hopefully believing - begging - it was a nightmare.

Around 7:20 that night we all embraced...tears flowing and shaking gasps filled the house...it wasn't quiet no more. I shrink back into the couch...back into my headphones hoping the soft lullaby would lure me away...an escape from this nightmare.

Denial

It's been months since the last time we spoke,
since I've seen you smile, laugh, yet
sometimes I forget for a moment and it's bliss
seeing pictures of you and reminiscing...

I saw a post today...it was an ad,
a cheesy one for a present for the coming holiday,
a simple trinket engrave with "I love you more"
just like the ones we would trade
back and forth - in a cycle
that should've never end...

I wish I could forget again.

Breathless

The walls are chipped showing the red hidden beneath.
The picture is off a bit in the corner.
The painting's leaning to the left.
The table's covered in fake candy fluff.

The lights flicker dragging me
deep into the ringing in my ears

There's dust on the floor.
When was the last time I swept?

it's passed seven now...
my stomach hurts
my breath hitches
as a door closes
and tears fall...
as I find myself
completely breathless.

Freely

I once told you that I missed you
with every fiber of my being...

I believed in every grip of your hands,
so soft and caring,
you would bounce back, be safe.
Healthy.

Now a fading...distance memory plays,
a sadist whim of my mind, your weak hands
grasping out, trembling, desperate for our warmth,
for the once-welcomed solace be ripped,
carved from the hearts we freely gave

It's not fair! After Everything...

I can still picture the steam-filled kitchen,
tea on the stove, roast in the crockpot,
music blasting where onions are sautéed
just for us as you smile big and say, "I love you more."

Anger

I want to scream. I want to yell.
I want to be angry....

even though I know it's for
the best....the raging pain
hidden in my chest
begs.

I'm tired of pretending...
I'm fine. I'm alright.
yet secretly I'm dying on the inside.

LET ME SCREAM
LET ME CRY OUT

Let me be angry this one time.

I've been thinking...

Thoughts racing, running rapid
against the steady pounding in my head -

How could you leave us?

The selfish thoughts dragging away ones of
your smile, your laugh...somehow always
featured in the kitchen - now left emptied.

How could you leave us?

I'm caught memorized by cooking bowls,
holiday (not for use) towels stuck against cabinets
like glue...all frozen in the lackluster lights
awaiting for your somber return
that never comes...

How could you leave us?

Doctors

It's on days like this when I miss your smile.
As you gently pat my shoulder and press a
small glass of hot tea in my hands.
"Everything will be alright." you would say
with some hidden wisdom in your eyes as
you take a seat next to me.

Yet the seat beside me remains empty with
only your past words flowing towards me,
ever so calming like before...but my hands
remain empty with the wish for your
kindness to once again wrap around me in
your warm embrace.

Anxiety clings to me hooking
its needled fingers into my heart tempting
my brain to give up...

To let the sinking teeth of anger to rip
through me. To seek revenge for their
thoughtless diagnosis that left you to wither
in agony. Years of suffering for such
stupidity and arrogance guiding those
sickening dicks in plastered smiles never

actually lifting a finger...never believing
only thinking...

Why did you have to die because men wouldn't believe
you?

Guilt

A deadly bile glides up my throat any time I try to take a bite. I think of your struggle with any food. I think of days you ate nothing which turned to months. A year. A lump grows in my throat. Does it feel similar to yours? The guilt tears at my throat, at my mind. I can't believe what you kept inside.

       And I can't believe I wasn't there for you.

A Simple Bookmark

I opened an old book today,
one that's been on my shelf for a while
and in it's pages was something that
reminded me of you.

A small bookmark hidden in the pages
of some small town romance...
just like all those movies we watched
together...

yet as I cling to these pages
I know that I would easily trade
them for just another second
with you every time.

Empty Chair

I don't want Christmas this year.
I don't want to wake up
cold, in the dark with no news on
at four or even six
trying to be patient, waiting
for the time to wake everyone up.

I don't want to sit in the dark
alone with nothing like anything before
as I try not to look at your empty
chair reminding me of the different
this year.

I don't want Christmas this year.
I just want you to be there.

Christmas Without You

I'm really worried about Christmas.
It's going to be so weird without
you there. It's going to be so hard
waking up without FOX playing on
the TV or having fresh coffee already
brewed. It's going to be weird not
having our hours long talks while
we wait until everyone wakes up.
It's going to be so weird opening
presents from you without being
able to hug you and say I love you.
Christmas isn't going to be the same
and I'm not okay with it.

Why does everyone expect me to fine...
Why can't I cry? Or be angry this time?
It's so unfair not to see you smiling
on your favorite day of the year...
why did you leave us so soon?
I don't know if I'm ready for
Christmas without you.

I love you,

I'll Grow My Hair Out For You

Do you remember a while back? I think it was around Thanksgiving when you asked me to grow my hair back out. You said I looked cute with it and that I should have some hair to go with my graduation cap in the spring. I laughed and playfully rolled my eyes because most of my hair was shaved off at the time. There was only a small bit of "fluff" I could run my fingers through, so I didn't really think you were serious, but I kept the thought in the back of my mind, *skipping that month's hair appointment...*

wasn't supposed to lead anywhere. It wasn't a grand gesture...it didn't have much thought...rather a lack of funds...yet as time went on and my hair grew...I couldn't help but smile and think of you...

The next time I saw you it was Christmas time...we were deep into our battles of "I love you more" and "No, I'm doing dishes." But you still made the sweet tea...extra sweet and always made sure I had a hot glass, my favorite way to drink it. Y'all even waited for me to hang the lights on the tree.... My favorite part of the holidays, decorating the tree with you, though I'm sorry I was a bit late. My exams took longer than I thought. At least the lights glowed bright during those nights. *Only a few...*

Short weeks past and along came the striking cold air... fierce to the skin...leaving me to freeze from head to toe clinging to a beanie as if it was my home...I decided to skip this hair appointment and just say no... (I was too cold...)

"You don't have to. I don't mind. Let me help you." I would say every time the dishes piled high in the sink or dusting became a thing. But without fail you would smile and say that's alright. Even when those Grinch lights hung far into the new year...Now I wonder if we got them down in time maybe things would be different...if we didn't wait. *I wish...*

I knew what I could say to you. I wish I had the power to turn back time... before the doctor visits... the harsh treatments that tore you apart only hoping they would build you back up... I wish...

I noticed how you changed. The sudden loss of appetite. The lack of color in your face. The dark circles underneath your eyes in the green glow of the Grinch lights. You didn't put up as much of a fight when I offered to help with dishes. I should've known then. You were sitting more...sleeping more...*and I wish...*

I could be there...from the first scan to this last one. To be there cheering you on through the good days... the bad days... and days when the sun seems to hide, and our pride remains only in your kind eyes.
But sadly, life has different plans.

Now I'm hundreds of miles away – guilt ridden- and only reading updates on Facebook...wondering if I should be afraid with every post, every call, every text I'm stuck waiting, debating whether it's alright to call... Is it the right time? Should I wake you? Will this be okay? Will this get better? I call out to some unknown power, A deity who can come and make everything better...*Yet the new...*

Scans aren't any better. Now you have new treatments I hear that give you a better chance against the raging pain in your chest.... though is it true? Doing this will make your fear appear? Will you lose more this time?

Remember my promise from last thanksgiving? Well, I never made it to a single appointment...and it's already passed my shoulders...even now I can picture your smile at the thought...But I wanted to ask you, with Christmas a few short months away and my love for short hair anyways…would you let me give you at least a piece of normalcy? Would you let me give back something that beast in your chest took away? *I'll…*

Gladly grow my hair out for you. So please don't cry and as time goes on and my hair grows out, I'll always smile and think of you with every glance toward a mirror.

I love you,

Overwhelmed

Some days it's hard to move. It's hard to think.
I'm overwhelmed, worried,
not sure how to help
just falling faster
not knowing how
or what to do....

Another Post

Another post on Facebook.
I figured by now I would be used to it.
Your old words once bubbling to lighten
one's day only now a cruel reminder of the
unfairness that life brings. Yet even as the
tears fall... I can't help and smile at the
memories you bring.

Reality

The droplets slide down the
clear glass... my eyes grow blurry
unfocused as the world falls silent
like my voice lost from the lump
in my throat - wishing to gasp out
scream, yet barley managing a
breath. My heart thumps aggressivly
as unwanted reality strikes
thunder rolls across the clouds...
in an instant our hearts were shattered
you were gone.

Melody

I can hear melody
sometimes a sweet whisper near my ear
lingering life a fairytale
other times a roar like a rapid tide
devouring me beneath it's waves
yet I can't help but know the melody
mixes against my heart playing on repeat
moving between my emotions while
secretly staying reminding me of you, of your hugs,
kind and sweet with strength unmatched by any-

And honestly I could use a sweet melody,
to be wrapped in your arms again.

Teaspoon

I found something yesterday
at the bottom of my silverware drawer
an old teaspoon you brought me before
engraved with "I love you more"
and a joking "I win" printed deep
into the curve.

It reminds me of us. Not related by
blood but a relationship engraved by life.

I was seven when I first met you
and you welcomed us with warm hugs
fresh food and much love.

I can't believe your gone...through
your hugs, your warmth,
and your kindness
you'll live on
with every little memory hidden
within a drawer and every teaspoon.

Acceptance?

I once read that acceptance is a stage of grief...
I'm not sure how that can be...
because I don't know how to accept this...
I don't think my family ever will
truly accept the loss of such a beautiful
soul like you...

Timeless Traditions

They're posting pictures again of your smile, a precious moment from your life... so many good times of traditions still appearing as a flag quietly raises late at night.

Small red tin creating years of your magic one last time sits on the shelf awaiting for secret late night treats.

Your love forever eternal within every picture captured and smiles caused by a simple mailbox of timelessness, past emotions.

May your love continue to live on, to grow long through the traditions and simple mailboxes. Your light, your magic will be missed this year.

Little Past Midnight

It's past midnight... I can't help but
wonder if you're alright.

Are you flying higher than you've
ever wanted...chasing clouds....
watching the sunset?

Free from all the aches of needles...
of constant wires wrapping around,
dressing you?

Are you happy now? Are you with
him? Smiling and laughing while
watching FOX with a pot on the
stove... waiting for us to someday
join you. It's a little past midnight...

Hand Mirror

Wow...it's already 2025...
Yet my brain still feels like 2020
Is shifting into a winter's breeze
Welcoming us into a New Year's kiss
And a hopeful embrace hidden in the folds
Of snowy blankets stretching out once again... I wonder
Will this year be kinder to us?
The onslaught of tears pool in my eyes
My throat tightens, and my hands grow cold
Yet they won't fall.
...because you wouldn't want that...
Locking myself in the past would do me no good.
I can hear you now...
"You're a writer, aren't you?"
...Telling me to write about it. (Is this what you meant?)
I remember you asking me
for a new story (I'll get to it...I swear!) ...
Just like you once asked me for longer hair...
To take better care of myself...
And to see what you saw in me...
You amazed me...
Your warm smile, generous heart
And brightening soul...accepting me without an ounce
of your blood running through my veins.

I'll take your words to heart
And start believing in myself
Just like you did until
I see what you see within
The mirror you gave me.
And yeah...I might as well try to finish that novel.
It's 2025 after all...new year, new me?
Hopefully, I'll believe in myself enough
To submit it this time
Just for you, so I can grow...
To be at least a bit like you come 2026
That is my goal.